SOUTHERN WAY   Special 1

S C TOWNROE'S JOURNEY IN STEAM

© Kevin Robertson (Noodle Books) Colour Rail, and R Blencowe 2014.
ISBN 978-1-909328-16-7
First published in 2014 by Kevin Robertson
under the **NOODLE BOOKS** imprint
PO Box 279
Corhampton
SOUTHAMPTON
SO32 3Z
www.noodlebooks.co.uk
editorial@thesouthernway.co.uk
Printed in England by
Berforts Information Press

Bincombe North tunnel (814 yards), with the north end seen top and south end below. At the north end is the signal box of the same name and the refuge siding for the banking engine between the up and down lines. The signal box had a frame with space for 13 levers although there was no No 10. The image was taken from the cab of a diesel. (CR 109865ST)

In the bottom view 'T9' No 30119 is running light towards Weymouth - the sand drag for up trains will be noted - and will soon be entering the shorter South Tunnel (56 yards). The lower view was recorded in May 1952.
(CR BRS1024)

Editorial Introduction

This is a book I have long wanted to undertake. Having been privileged to meet the late Stephen Townroe on several occasions and similarly view some of his photographic collection, I felt a volume just on his work was long overdue. Unfortunately time always seemed to be against me but as years passed I have come to realise if I don't get around to it now I perhaps never will. Consequently with generous access provided to his photographic collection by Rod Blencowe and Paul Chancellor, it was almost a case of 'now or never' - so here goes!

How the interest in the material came about can be traced back to my first meeting with the man, now over 25 years ago, but something I still recall vividly.

At the time I was working on the first edition of my book on 'Leader' (subsequently published by Alan Sutton). I happened to remark to Bill Bishop that I really wanted to know more about the time the engine spent on trial at Eastleigh and he suggested I should see Mr Townroe. I immediately considered it to be an excellent suggestion, but Bill was quick to counter this with the words, "..don't tell him I sent you…", said in a way as to imply both fear and respect for a man who I knew had run Eastleigh shed with the proverbial rod of iron for some years. Even so I was also advised he was 'fair', I could ask for no more.

Finding him was not difficult, Bill knew he had retired to a cottage at Upham. I knew I had arrived at the right place as stood in the porch was a nameplate from 'Lord Collingwood'. I knocked to be greeted by a diminutive man but one with a firm voice. His immediate repost was, "Who are you - what do you want?". I had been warned of his manner and replied, "Bill Bishop suggested I should come and see you" (ignoring the request Bill had said that his name not be mentioned). There was a further blunt, "Well, what about?" - I could never have said he was not straight and to the point. "About this" I replied, and with my hand which had been up to that time hidden behind my back, I produced a view of No 36001.

The response was immediate, a grunt followed by the words "You'd better come in then."

That then was my first meeting with the redoubtable Stephen Collingwood Townroe, and who I like to think having established that my intentions were genuine, could not have been more helpful.

I made several visits after that time, even being allowed to borrow some of his valuable colour slides which he graciously allowed me to copy. Indeed no question I ever asked, about 'Leader' or indeed any other railway subject, was ever ignored. What I did notice though was that he would never elaborate, sticking solely to the facts of his answer. Oh how I now wish I had asked him so much more. Here was a man, who, I have learned since, was apprenticed at Vulcan Foundry, Newton-le-Willows and then joined the Southern Railway in 1932. The following year he was a Head Office junior or 'runner' under the locomotive Running Superintendent and visited every depot from Ramsgate to Wadebridge. He recalled that some of the shedmasters whose depots he visited were rather 'stuck up' and not helpful. This was put down to them having belonged to the pre-1923 companies and thus suspicious of new faces.

His subsequent career is referred to on the next pages including his first management role as Shed Foreman (the title 'Shedmaster' was a BR term) at Dorchester in 1938 where he also acted as relief to R D Steele, the latter in charge of the parent depot at Bournemouth. Later he was engaged with war work both on the SR and on at least one occasion on the LMS. There was also a period spent assisting at Nine Elms although the dates for this move are not reported. During BR days he was at Eastleigh and when he left was presented with one of the nameplates from No 30862 'Lord Collingwood', hence the nameplate seen at the time of my first visit.

A few years later I had a special reason to thank 'SCT' for his help. My ongoing research into 'Leader' had, unbeknown to me, touched a few nerves elsewhere. So much so that I received a telephone call from a retired railwayman whose name would be well known to students of SR history, but who spent some time both berating my efforts at research whilst ending up with threats of legal action should my book ever be published.

I confided in Mr Townroe. As ever he was short and to the point. "Leave him to me" was all he said. I never heard another word from my critic, 'SCT' in the meanwhile also agreed to write a foreword to the book.

I have never mentioned this story in print up to now but in attempting a photographic biography of his collection now is the time for it to be made public.

Speaking to former Eastleigh men it would be fair to say he was certainly respected, but then he was also in charge of a cross-section of humanity, his task being to get the best out of the men and machines under his control. Other snippets from his life are referred to in narrative and captions that follow.

I can imagine working for him he would indeed have been a hard taskmaster. What of course has only come out in recent years is how much of an enthusiast he also was, his position allowed him access to locations and incidents barred to other, lesser mortals.

It has been a privilege to put together this small tribute, none of which would have been possible without the help of the Townroe family. To me as an outsider he was a man who immediately came across as 'Southern' through and through and also one to whom I owe special debt of thanks.

Kevin Robertson   *Hampshire 2014*

Front cover - *No 35020 'Bibby Line' outside Salisbury shed in June 1956 and complete with dynamometer car. The original rather than rebuilt tender will be noted - see full details pages 10/11. (CR BRS1007)*

Rear cover - *A rare colour view of the cab of 'U' class 2-6-0 No 1790 at Yeovil in 1939, a right-hand drive engine with much of the brass and copper suitably burnished. (CR 312066)*

S C TOWNROE'S JOURNEY IN STEAM

In preparing this brief portrait of Stephen Townroe, I was always aware of how little I knew of the man himself. True, I had met him on several occasions but that was twenty years earlier and at that time I had asked him specific questions, which were always answered with courtesy.

I now wanted to know more about the man himself. I was certain there was story to uncover and to tell and yet for some time all my enquiries seemed to lead to dead-ends, little it seemed ever having appeared in print.

On the theme of railway history there have been innumerable biographies and autobiographies written either about or by railway staff. They were men who had either occupied a position at the very top or a lowly one on the career ladder, leaving under-represented the men in the middle.

Fortunately that omission was put right following a visit to Oxford. Here I spent a most interesting time with Judi, one of the Townroe daughters. I was able to establish that 'Pa' had in fact recorded a brief discourse on his career, while Judi was able to fill in the gaps as well provide an insight into his early life and describe the type of man he was.

It has been a privilege to work on this book. I only hope the results will do justice to a man who created (and still leaves) an impression twenty years after his passing.

Kevin Robertson

(Quotes are from a brief handwritten discourse on his own life, kindly made accessible by the Townroe family. Some of these relate to his activities away from the railway but are well worthy of inclusion to give a flavour of life of the time.)

Stephen Collingwood Townroe (SCT) was born into an Edwardian family at his grandparents home, Mere House, Newton-le-Willows in 1911. The eldest of four children. His father Bernard Stephen Townroe was secretary of the Franco-British Society was well as having wide experience in public affair, as a JP, architect, journalist and later, Mayor of Hampstead from 1934 to 1936.

In his early years he recalls being looked after by a nanny, whilst school holidays were later spent with both sets of grandparents. Indeed his maternal grandfather, William Collingwood, besides being recalled as a comic by his grandchildren, would be destined to exhibit much influence on young Stephens's later career choice. He was educated at Bickley Hall School and then Eastbourne College, where he was a boarder by the age of 10.

At Eastbourne he was a gifted pupil but admits he quickly become bored with Latin and Greek. To while away the time (when he perhaps should have been paying rather more attention to the classics), he produced a schedule of movements between each part of the school. This was in the form of a railway timetable, his comment being, "I would imagine I was driving a train between classes." He was also a boxer – something which would prove useful on one occasion during his apprenticeship!

Having left Eastbourne, his father hoped he might have followed in his own footsteps and go to Oxford. Indeed SCT's enjoyment of all things sporting may well have come from his father, who had rowed during his own time at St John's College.

Stephen Townroe c1947.

4

Stephen's ambitions though lay elsewhere and when it became apparent that he had inherited his grandfather Collingwood's aptitude for engineering, it was arranged that he would serve a term of five years as a Pupil at the Vulcan Foundry starting in September 1929. Lodgings were arranged for him in Cross Lane East, Newton-le-Willows. In his own words "I took my work seriously at Vulcan and was well tutored by some of the older men, foremen, fitters, moulders, pattern-makers etc. who had known my family. One day per week I went to Manchester on part time day courses in mechanical engineering at Manchester School of Technology. Everyone worked like beavers and the tutors gave enough homework to occupy all my evenings except Saturdays and Sundays."

Vulcan Foundry was where William Collingwood had been Works Manager and later Managing Director. As MD, Grandfather would leave for work daily at 09.00, collected by the chauffeur from the family's Victorian country house set in three acres near Newton-le-Willows. As a Gentleman within the community William Collingwood was a Justice of the Peace and Chairman of the Urban District Council. When time permitted, he also enjoyed cycling, which his grandson would later emulate, culminating in the related cycling pocket book in 1974. (Grandfather had retired by the time a young Stephen Townroe arrived at Vulcan's and the Works was now run by an Uncle, Gerald Collingwood.)

At Vulcan Foundry, SCT recalls there was a black shunting engine at the Works named 'Marjorie', in his autobiography he recalled it as , 'black and unimpressive, a four-wheeler'. No doubt the machine had been named by his Grandfather in honour of his daughter, SCT's mother but there any similarity ended, for Marjorie Townroe (née Collingwood) was a renowned beauty and former debutante.

Even though Grandfather was no longer in charge at Vulcan, he was still regarded as something of a deity – he was all-seeing and all-knowing. Any jobs that were spoiled and thus discarded for scrap were investigated, whilst he would regularly ask the cause and seek out the culprit.

Two specific incidents are recalled during the time SCT spent at Vulcan. The first was when a batch of locomotives for the Argentine Railways and gauged to their 5' 6" track width were, for the first time, moved complete by road from Newton-le-Willows to Liverpool. Previously the new engines had been dismantled but there was now a shipping line with vessels capable of taking the engines fully assembled. Even so, moving them was not without incident as the weight of the loads caused much damage to the roads, especially underground pipes. SCT had witnessed some of these moves by following on his motorcycle. (Somewhat proudly he also commented that his engineering training had given him the skills to maintain and repair machines of all types, including when necessary, the motorcycle.)

The second incident occurred during his pupilage when he was serving in the 'automatic machine shop'. 'Pupils' were identified by a white collar (not ideal wear for an engineering works) which

was "spoiled by an older man throwing an oily rag at me. I went over and clouted him, with the result that he was knocked out and had to be taken to the ambulance room. The foreman reported the incident and my Uncle, Works manager at the time, felt he had to act and I was suspended for three days – I learned afterwards that Uncle was in fact rather pleased that I had shown the ability of one of the 'privileged apprentices' to exercise a little authority and stick up for myself."

Time passed. SCT went on, "At Vulcan I learned some of the facts of life from which I had been shielded previously. I made many friends and few enemies." Unfortunately came the great slump of 1931 and with it a cessation of orders. Most of the 3,000 workforce was laid off, those who had previously worn bowler hats now donning overalls and overhauling the works machinery simply for something to do. SCT was similarly affected in that, at the time, he had yet to have work experience of the Erecting Shop, Boiler Shop and Drawing Office, all of which was now impossible.

Fortunately an arrangement existed between Vulcan and the LNER whereby both pupil and privileged apprentices could go to Gorton locomotive shed for "operating" experience. Accordingly he was sent there in 1931, moving to some new lodgings with an out of work musician in Newton Street, Openshaw. As he wrote at the time, "Gorton and Openshaw were dull, drab dirty suburbs of Manchester. The locomotive depot was surrounded by high walls on which political slogans were painted. But I was fascinated by the rows of locomotives in the shed, many in steam and waiting for the next duty; here the locomotive becomes a live thing and it was not long before I was driving them up and down the sidings, and tinkering with them as a fitter; the latter caused a little difficulty for me with a trade union, as I didn't belong".

It was his experiences at Gorton that caused him to write what may have been his very first article, although unfortunately it cannot be traced. Gorton also had another result, for following the completion of their training, men would choose to take either the workshop or operating routes. SCT chose the latter but to achieve this he would have to join a railway company. At the time the decision was well founded. Whilst the risk of unemployment remained high, the railway companies, "although offering modest salaries, afforded greater security when one got 'on the staff'".

By now Uncle Gerald had also left Vulcan and was working on the South Indian Railway. There was the possibility SCT would follow in the same tradition – his Grandfather had also spent time overseas as an engineer – but Uncle Gerald expressed a note of caution in that senior posts were more and more being given to native officials and the chances of a responsible post were lessening year by year.

India's loss was to be the Southern Railway's gain, as eventually (September 1932) Bernard Townroe accompanied his son to an interview with R E L Maunsell. The result was a continuation of the pupilage and more experience in the area missed at Newton-le-Willows with the additional element of costing experience. Again SCT created a favourable impression, for after spending a

The first railway book published in 1947. The contents were black and white and included both Southern and Great Western subjects. (The reference 'No 6' referred to what was the sixth book in the series, other similar volumes having been compiled by other photographers using their own material.)

final month at Ashford, Maunsell stated he could remain with the Southern, an opportunity not afforded to all pupils who had completed their time.*

Before leaving Manchester for Eastleigh, SCT had sat his HNC exams in mechanical engineering. As a result of this we now witness a rare show of pride, for he comments, " I passed with distinction – much to my surprise." Maunsell also made it known that unless a pupil or premium apprentice became a graduate member of the IMechE he could not expect any recommendation for continuing employment. Consequently in 1933 only two who had completed their training were retained, Gordon Nicholson and Stephen Townroe.

With the Southern his first proper job was at Waterloo in 1933, as junior to A D Jones the Locomotive Running Superintendent. Again we only have a veiled hint of the nature of his work in the department, although this included various 'errands and investigations' at all the Southern locomotive depots from Ramsgate to Wadebridge. Brought up in the steam era, there then followed a poignant comment, for at this stage in his memoirs he adds, "Now, in 1967, almost all are closed or converted to other purposes."

At the time he also rode on engines of every type as well as all the express workings. For one week his duty involved the 'Golden Arrow' for the purpose of checking carriage heating about which there had been a high level of complaints. There was also some time spent on the 'Schools' class specifically between London and Ramsgate trying out various alterations and settings of the springing. The engines having been reported as 'lively' at higher speeds. Townroe recalls his chief (whether Jones or Maunsell is unclear), as being still very nervous following the

derailment of the 'River' class engine at Sevenoaks in 1927. Consequently reports of 'lively riding' by the 'Schools' were promptly investigated.

Travelling on steam engines should not, however, be always guaranteed a pleasurable experience. He recalls being ill with ear trouble after a cold day spent on a goods engine between Willesden and Hither Green. When he returned to duty, his first task was to, "examine the turntable at West Worthing". He duly set off only to find the turntable had been removed sometime previously. He comments that he spent the rest of the day enjoying the sea air at Worthing!

There was also work involved in assisting with the movement of special race trains to and from Ascot as well as other special workings destined for the Aldershot Military Tattoo and arriving from all parts. The experience the Southern built up in regulating and despatching traffic to so many destinations would prove invaluable in the subsequent evacuation from Dunkirk.

In 1934 he was moved from Waterloo to the Carriage Works at Eastleigh, where he took on the role of 'Progress Assistant' to the Works Manager. Eastleigh was then involved in a very heavy programme of new electric trains for the services to Portsmouth, Alton, Gillingham and Maidstone. As already noted, a works appointment was clearly not to his liking for he adds, "This proved to be a dull and thankless task, going round the works every day chasing the shop foremen and dealing with lists of hundreds of parts." Even so, he was philosophical when he added, " But it was an appointment not to be spurned, for it was a step up the ladder." Whilst at Eastleigh he lodged at South Stoneham House, part of Southampton University's accommodation.

Relief from the tedium of the carriage works came with his motorcycle outings (but no longer the machine he rode at Manchester) and on which he explored "much of the South of England."

Matters improved in 1936 when he transferred to the Locomotive Works as a 'Progress Engineer'. This was a more technical appointment and dealt with the standards of repair and the testing of locomotives.

A further change came in 1937 when Alan Cobb (who had replaced A D Jones as Locomotive Running Superintendent at Waterloo) wanted a Technical Assistant to deal with the maintenance of locomotives in service and take control of the 35 locomotive depots. SCT started in this role in September of that year. Munich brought a new challenge including staff being instructed in the wearing of gas masks. "We had to pass through a room full of tear gas." The memories of 1914-1918 were clearly still uppermost in people's minds.

Away from the political situation, there is reference to the "lesser task" of organising new speed recorders, which were fitted to various types of express engine. The results were recorded on a paper roll and scrutinised to see whether any driver was exceeding speed limits. The experiment was dropped on the outbreak of war, "but not before speeds of over 100 mph had been achieved, to which a blind eye was turned by us!")

Something of the life of the time may be gauged in the comment that in January 1938 he became a member of the Southern Railway Superannuation Fund: a sign that "one had arrived". Even so, his annual salary was still only £200 *per annum*. He adds, "My last motorcycle, a brand-new AJS costing £30 had been a gift from Granny Collingwood.....it was really only interest and not the salary that kept me working for the railway".

In November 1938 came the first of what we might call management appointments, taking charge of the depot at Dorchester. Lodgings were at a guest house where one of the other occupants was the Master of the Cattistock Hunt. SCT's skills with his Leica camera led to an invitation to take a series of pictures of the hunt and he travelled over many areas of Dorset following the hounds. He then returns to his railway role, "I had a faithful clerk, Monty Northam, who looked after things when I was away."

Just six months later, in April 1939, came a move to Yeovil together with a salary raise of £20 p.a. Initially sorry to leave Dorchester, he quickly warmed to his new appointment, also recalling that he was in the depot in September 1939 when Neville Chamberlain's famous Munich speech was broadcast. (This also goes to show why he recorded the arrival of the various evacuation trains at Yeovil as depicted in 'SW Special No 3 – Wartime Southern'.) It was also at Yeovil that he refers to having to deal "with a "bit of a smash up which I had to clear up". Unfortunately there is no elaboration and a search of available records for 1939 provides no further information.

The outbreak of war caused another move, this time to the Southern's wartime headquarters at Deepdene with responsibility for the locomotive department's air raid precautions and fire fighting. As time went on so this brief extended and eventually covered virtually anything placed on his shoulders including locomotive repairs, War Department engines for use overseas, coal reserves and even manpower . It was around this time that SCT's skills also came to fore as he made a 'photographic copier' by which the staff records of 10,000 men were put on to microfilm and kept securely in a cave.

Some relief from war came when he married Esme Holland in September 1942, for until that time he had literally worked and slept at Deepdene with a roving commission to visit every depot on the Southern. Esme was the daughter of medical missionaries then working in Pakistan. From 1943, home was a rented bungalow in Portway Crescent, Ewell. (This accommodation only came about through the intercession of Alan Cobb. There was an acute housing shortage but the Southern railway agreed to purchase the property on condition that rent was paid at 4% of the purchase price.) It was here that the Townroe twins, Judith and Mary spent their early years. The family would be complete with Rosemary's arrival a few years later.

SCT refers to his time at Deepdene as 'interesting'. We know he was involved in trials involving the re-railing of a locomotive by a crew wearing full gas mask protection at Drumclog, Ayrshire – see 'Wartime LMS' by L G Warburton, published by Noodle Books. There was also the time he spent riding LNER 'A4' Pacifics, which were being lubricated with a substitute oil as the 'rape' component was no longer available following Japanese control of the Far East. He recalls having to take the temperature of various bearings at regular intervals. (On this topic, Norman McKillop in his 'Enginemen Elite' published by Ian Allan is a good reference.)

SCT also speaks of the difficulty of maintaining 1,600 engines in service and it was only after long arguments with the Ministry of Labour that it was finally accepted that skilled fitters could not be drafted into the forces without serious consequences for railway movement.

At Deepdene there was a railway control room with direct lines of communication to the Admiralty, War Office and Air Ministry. Requirements for special trains would arrive needing immediate action, including one where he himself organised a special train for Mr Churchill. The departure point and train destination are not mentioned. Security was such that all non-essential personnel were prohibited from being on the platform but that did not prevent SCT from secreting Esme nearby. For the rest of her life she recalled the occasion, especially as Mr Churchill had turned to her, giving one of his famous 'V for Victory' signs.

Another difficulty was bombing which rendered lines impassable and called for diversions. Key staff – and here he specifically mentions drivers – might also find their homes bombed and alternative accommodation was only possible in a totally different area with consequent difficulties in travelling to work. A

The Guildford role was not really that of Shed Foreman, instead the appointment title was 'Assistant Divisional Locomotive Superintendent, Western Division based at Woking but with responsibility for Guildford'. In overall charge was E S Moore but again it was only a short-term move, as by 1947 he moved to Exeter replacing Jock Rogers, who transferred to Headquarters. Unfortunately politics now intruded, for the Exeter appointment caused some difficulties on the part of another who claimed seniority. The appeal was also upheld with the result that the transfer was revised to a similar role at Eastleigh. As a result, the family moved to another railway owned property, in Shanklin Road, Southampton.

The impression is now gained that he might initially have been somewhat wary over the Eastleigh move, although we are not told why. Instead he adds, "Like many other setbacks, the move to Eastleigh proved better than the Exeter job in many ways."

Change, however, was in the air, for within two years of nationalisation a new promotional scheme covering the whole of the network opened up and with it the opportunity for senior men from other areas to move to the South of England. Understandably a degree of bitterness creeps in, for he adds "… my prospects naturally suffered as I had been 'groomed' for the top jobs on the Southern which were now filled from outside." Later, a reorganisation of motive power posts took place with the Southern Region split into six districts, with any senior men naturally displaced by those appointed to those six district jobs. At Eastleigh the effect was to give him a new title, 'Assistant Motive Power Superintendent under Will Nicholson'. Fortunately Nicholson lived at Guildford and had made it clear he had no intention of working at Eastleigh. The result was that SCT took all the calls – hence he was seen out and about at derailments, invariably with his camera – whilst Nicholson was also averse to dictating letters, also dealt with at Eastleigh. SCT adds, "We got on very well"

A year later, Woking District was re-graded with the Superintendent and his assistant being given an additional £100 p.a., justified on the basis that theirs was in fact a busier district than Eastleigh's, although in fact it had fewer locomotives and the trains were, in the main, electric. SCT adds that if this had taken place in 1950 he would have benefited and could have taken one of the roles. As it was, the vacancy was now filled by a man brought in from the LMR.

Notwithstanding any difficulties affecting his own career, it was evident that Townroe was also held in high regard by those at (or who had been at) the very top. An example of this came in 1950 with the trials of No 36001 – the infamous 'Leader'. This locomotive, having failed to live up to its expectations, the British Railways Board was determined to decide, one way or the other, the future of the machine. Bulleid had by now moved to Ireland (where he was already planning 'Leader V2', to be known as the 'Turfburner') but somehow his message got out, "Send it to Eastleigh – Townroe will sort it out". And notwithstanding Townroe's later comments to the present writer on his views over the Bulleid breed, it cannot be said that SCT was anything other than totally professional in the way he

In 1947 he compiled 'Practical Hints for Footplate Men' to be followed later by his joint authorship of 'Handbook for Railway Steam Locomotive Enginemen'. The photograph shows an example of firing an original 'Bulleid' locomotive.

Government grant enabled the provision of depot canteens, the organisation of which partly fell to him, including obtaining the necessary food rationing permits. It was a difficult time and one can probably imagine the relief he must have felt when, once more, he was given charge of a depot, this time at Guildford early in 1945.

organised a trial crew to work the engine. (The full story of No 36001, including its tests from Eastleigh, are told in 'The Leader Project: Fiasco or Triumph' by Kevin Robertson, published by Ian Allan.)

What was destined to be his first spell at Eastleigh was destined to be limited, as by 1954 he had moved back to Woking as Assistant DMPS which role also included a period of night work in the control office, going by car to Woking, "…and stopping *en route* on Pirbright Common to hear the chiming of the night jars."

By 1956 he had moved to Waterloo as Mechanical Assistant to the Motive Power Superintendent, in which role he comments, "The newly-modified Pacifics were then just entering service and I had an interesting job in organising the maintenance of them – and all the 1500 odd locos – and having small design changed made as a result of the trials". The Waterloo Motive Power Superintendent was T E (Tommy) Chrimes, SCT recalling that, "…he did not interfere with me very much." Once a week his duties took him to Brighton to meet the Shopping Bureau Manager and discuss repairs of locomotives at works. Although there was a direct route through Redhill and Haywards Heath to Brighton he instead chose to travel 'the pretty way' via Guildford, Cranleigh, Christ's Hospital and Steyning – hence the colour images later in this book.

The job also involved visiting all the steam depots so living at Farnham was therefore an ideal centre from which to cover the Southern both east and west. He also recalls with sadness the death of his Chief Inspector, Ted Dibb, whom he had personally selected from Scotland.

SCT returned to Eastleigh in 1957, after Gordon Thompson the Eastleigh DMPS was found dead on board his houseboat. At the time, reorganisation was yet again in the air and the post, rather than permanent was designated 'Acting'. It was at this stage that his daily 'commute' involved travel on the Alton line trains – hence again the colour illustration later.

It is easy to imagine the frustration that ensued, for nine months passed still without any indication of the role becoming permanent. Eventually the opportunity arose for a personal discussion with C P Hopkins, the Southern Region's General Manager and which followed one of his monthly conferences. Hopkins was sympathetic and although some further time elapsed, eventually he was confirmed in the Eastleigh role and in consequence of some house-hunting, the family moved to 'Colleton' at Shawford.

Eastleigh Motive Power District covered some 70 route miles of main, secondary and branch lines, around 2,000 men, some 350 locomotives and various sub-depots. It was recalled as a 'happy district'. "We had our arguments but never any bad blood. The men knew I was their best advocate when in trouble and seldom appealed when I punished." What no doubt helped was that SCT was seen not just as 'the boss' but someone who would come out on the road with his men. Consequently he rode on both steam and diesel "…and did a bit of driving." There were also numerous social occasions .

The Hampshire dieselisation scheme was implemented during his tenure and he made a point of personally addressing the drivers at the start of each 3-week training course. Two Inspectors, Messrs Pope and Stephens were also involved. Notwithstanding the new traction he was able to instil a pride in the job and failures were few.

In 1961 he was given the chance of promotion to Woking but considered it unattractive. Partly this was due to labour relations in the London area being difficult whilst the lure of an additional £100 was insufficient to justify the move. In his own words, "The family comes first."

Further reorganisation in 1962 saw the formation of 'Divisions' and eventually it became clear his 'District' was to be absorbed. The opportunity came for a job as District Traffic Superintendent at Southampton but without warning this was suddenly filled by someone from outside. Change was now almost continuous with a move to the role of 'Movements Officer' at Southampton. Senior management seemed unwilling – or perhaps unable – to explain the future, although eventually he was given the role of 'District Manager' at Southampton but again only in an 'acting' capacity. This time it appeared it was the British Railways Board who was promoting change with the former 'districts' being replaced by 'areas'.

One thing we do know is that in 1962 he was presented with one of the nameplates from withdrawn 'Lord Nelson' No 30862 'Lord Collingwood', a group of Eastleigh cleaners having the task of removing the plate from the engine. Unfortunately no photographs of the presentation have been found and the plate was sold by the family some years later.

Reading SCT's words from the time, there is a clear sense of understandable frustration at this point. After all here was a man who was highly qualified, skilled and experienced and yet underused. Mention by name is made of senior men from the time, who, from his autobiography, appeared to be unsympathetic to anyone from the steam era. The world had moved on, made clear when his chief, F B Taylor, suggested he apply for the job of Area Manager at Southampton even though this was at a lower salary. We are not told if he actually did apply, although in the event BRB made the appointment of a younger man from the Western Region. In January 1966 he recognised his own frailty as far as the railway was concerned, "I was superfluous". There was an exchange of personal letters with the General Manager which drew the response that, "…he was 'so sorry', people like me were redundant but 'something would be found to my liking'". Of course this was the time when steam had only a short time to survive, there was simply no need for an operational steam man like Stephen Townroe.

In the event he settled into a new role following a meeting with the Chief Mechanical and Electrical Engineer, Arnold Sykes. Together with former Eastleigh Works Manager Charles Shepherd, their job was to chase up the rolling stock in order to be ready for the Bournemouth Electrification, originally intended to 'go live' on 31 December 1966. This date though proved ambitious and steam repairs had to be reinstated at Eastleigh in the autumn of 1966 so as to have the chance of maintaining any

'SCT' in his office at Eastleigh. The offices and what had formerly been enginemen's dormitories were located under the water tank at Eastleigh with the windows facing south. Depicted here is the man responsible for the main depot at Eastleigh plus its sub-sheds. This included 350 locomotives, 2,000 men and locomotive operation on 70 route miles of main, cross-country and branch line. On the wall behind are heraldic shields from the former constituents of the Southern Railway. After he had retired the present author asked SCT of his opinions on Bulleid. The reply was straightforward but given on the condition it would not be publicised until after his death, (referring to the 'Leader' locomotive that had given SCT so much trouble at Eastleigh in 1950), " Bulleid soon left BR to become CME of CIE in Ireland. It was a revelation of Bulleid's ways of thinking that he proceeded to repeat his mistakes with a similar design to No 36001, except that this time he put the enginemen in a separate cab. It was an experiment which the Irish railways could not afford and it, too, had to be scrapped, without earning a penny or a punt. Such blindness to reality was inexplicable. Bulleid was clever, self-centred, ingenious charming with equals but inconsiderate and supercilious towards his underlings...he was a cold fish, he was erratic….he was in workshops all his life. He had no first-hand experience as a District Traffic or Motive Power Officer. He did not discuss his design ideas with the users….hence nobody warned him that the inside of the Leader would be unbearable. Bulleid did not like people with practical experience and I am convinced that was why he did not talk about the MN design with my chief in 1939, nor about the Bleeder in 1946. Now that he has passed away, I think the truth about him can be written without any offence, and of course without malice.

Photo courtesy the Townroe family.

form of service. As SCT put it, "…we were watchdogs and would bark only when necessary. Our barks were also polite."

He concludes his writing with a short sentence (referring to the eventual start of the Bournemouth electrification in July 1967 – a delay of seven months), "The trains started on 10 July, with no margin to spare."

His final role was at Woking but with the ending of his own writing, we have little clear idea what this involved. He appears not to have kept a daily work diary so we do not know the details of his day-to-day activities in any of his respective roles, nor do we know of any incidents or occasions in which he may have been involved apart from the evidence provided by his many

photographs, dating back to around 1938, both colour and black and white. That he was present is something which had always been suspected but which can now be now confirmed, given the accompanying caption details of the locations and the dates of the photographs.

Probably one of the happiest times of his career was in the two spells he had at Eastleigh, a big depot, a big area and with the opportunity to run his portion of the railway the way he felt it should. As regards the engines themselves, I recall discussions with him in which he promoted the work of Maunsell, which was compared favourably with Bulleid. When I asked why, his explanation was as ever, simple and straight to the point, "A Maunsell engine is predictable. Providing the crew is willing and the coal is good, it will give the same performance day in and day out. A Bulleid might be exceptional on one day but it is unreliable and, without any change, will be totally different tomorrow. That is no good for me when trying to run a regular service." We may assume he was referring to the original Bulleids, although I did not press the point. This was also one of the reasons why he had all sixteen members of the 'Lord Nelson' class transferred to Eastleigh: they were reliable performers which the men could also get used to.

Stephen Townroe retired a few years later. Again we have a glimpse into the frustration that he must have experienced in his final working years this time from a letter he wrote to Roy Steele - a man who had occupied similar positions on the Southern Railway and later the Southern Region but had retired due to ill health in 1960. He describes the 1960s as follows, "There was not much pleasure with the deterioration of steam, broken down engines driven by men without the pride drivers took in pre -1939 days…..nobody at Marylebone had any time for steam, or officers brought up in steam".

This last sentence probably also summed up his frustration. He had given the railway his all, but the 'new' railway now had no place for a man with his background.

Without the responsibilities of work, he could turn his attention to recreational pastimes. He was resourceful putting his family first, as, (quoting from Judi), "… a hunter-gatherer…..he used to be a first-class wild fruits and vegetable picker! I remember him finding potatoes growing on the cliffs near Mudeford on holiday and us bringing them proudly back for lunch!" He also became skilled as a restorer of antique furniture, especially chairs. He was also an accomplished artist, talented musician and knowledgeable ornithologist.

There was also an outlet for his writings, as, apart from that first recollection of Gorton in earlier years, he had contributed to 'The Railway Gazette' and 'Meccano Magazine', in the latter guise sometimes under his own name and sometimes using the pseudonym 'Shedmaster'. His first railway book was a small paperback in the series 'My Best Railway Photographs', after which came 'The Book of the Schools Class', 'The King Arthurs and Lord Nelsons of the Southern Railway', 'The Bulleid Pacifics of the Southern' – with Cecil J Allen, and then his masterly 'Arthurs, Nelsons and Schools at Work'. All his railway books were published by Ian Allan. Together with Dick Tydesley (ex LMS) and Dick Robson (ex LNER), he was also responsible for the standard work of reference 'Handbook for Railway Steam Locomotive Enginemen', the latter still referred to by enginemen working on today's heritage lines.

One other book might also be mentioned for in 1974 he wrote 'How to Mend your Bike' – aimed at a younger generation but clearly showing the engineer in him was still to the fore. He was evidently delighted when he discovered a copy had been found in West Africa.

During his time in retirement he was approached by Ron White who had established the firm of 'Colour Rail' to preserve and make available colour slides. Some examples from SCT's camera had of course already be seen in print but the majority of the colour material remained hidden from general view. Ron White

recalls making the initial approach at the suggestion of another railway notary, R N H 'Dick' Hardy, who had commented. "...there might be something there worth looking at…" Initially sceptical Ron was soon accepted and a rapport established which allowed the prized material to be saved for posterity.

To his men 'SCT' was undoubtedly 'the boss', a stickler for punctuality but also a man who recognised and was appreciative of hard work put in by others. As a result he was probably loved or otherwise in equal measure, but certainly respected.

To those others he met, he extended courtesy but he similarly expected respect in return. To his children he was simply 'Pa'. Stephen Townroe made a final house move to Shaftesbury, from where he had a view for miles across Blackmore Vale. He died in 1991 aged 81, survived by his wife Esme, his three daughters and seven grandchildren.

Further black and white images taken by Stephen Townroe, depicting some of his railway experiences in wartime together with subsequent breakdown work have been included in, 'Southern Way Special No 5: Wartime Southern Part 2', 'Southern Way Special No 8: The Other Side of the Southern', and 'LMS Wartime', all published by Noodle Books. 'On Didcot, Newbury & Southampton Lines' published by Ian Allan, includes a number of his colour images from this railway.

THREE COLOURS FOR THE MERCHANT NAVY CLASS

The original Merchant Navy class locos have worn five colours during their lifetime. As built, the first few engines appeared in photographic grey - whether this applied to every member of the type is not certain - but what is confirmed is that within a short space of time this grey had given over to wartime black relieved only by 'sunshine' lettering and the various brass embellishments in the form of name and number plates plus the circular 'Southern' ring adorning the smokebox.

With a return to peace, SR Malachite appeared, several engines later sporting a combination of British Railways ownership and numbering allied to pre-nationalisation colours. Later, certain members of the class appeared in the then standard blue livery intended for express passenger types, the final colour being BR Brunswick green. Examples of all three are shown here.

Opposite top - No 35011 is captured emerging from Eastleigh Works for trials, probably in September 1948. 'General Steam Navigation' had been restored to green SR livery in January 1947. Whether what is seen is an initial light engine trial, usually to either Micheldever or Botley, or the engine was now destined for the running shed and a return to its home depot at Nine Elms is not reported. (CR BRS1000)

Opposite bottom - No 35024 was recorded in April 1950 with nameplate 'East Asiatic Company' covered until the time of formal unveiling. (Naming was at Waterloo on 5 May 1949.) As built in November 1948, the engine had appeared in malachite green but was repainted in blue with three crimson lines, blue wheels and skirting in February 1949. A month later the crimson lines had been replaced with black lines edged in white, whilst the front skirting was also now black. The final change to that seen, involving the black continuing below the cab and along the lower edge of the tender, took place in April 1949, this also now became the standard livery for the class. The engine was recorded leaving Eastleigh Works. (CR BRS1008)

Above - Standard BR Brunswick green for No 35027 'Port Line' seen at Victoria in March 1954. (CR BRS379)

REBUILDING A BULLEID

Eastleigh Works 1956 'Rebuilding a Bulleid'. S C Townroe recorded these three views as having been taken at Eastleigh in 1956, possibly depicting No 35014 'Nederland Line' - the reason for this supposition is that all four slides are consecutively numbered - Nos 1015417 to 105420. Even so they would have been taken at slightly differing periods. (The locomotives behind and alongside may be identified as Nos 34030 and 34041.) With the lack of staff visible it is likely the images were taken on a Sunday, whilst the name of the Erecting Shop foreman is also indicated from his ladder propped against the frame. In the view top left, the new smokebox saddle and middle cylinder are visible, whilst bottom left the view is from the centre of the frame looking towards the front. On this page work has progressed with cylinder covers and valves added whilst the painters have also been busy.
(CR 105417ST / 105418ST / 105419ST)

No 35014 spent some weeks at Eastleigh from mid-May until the start of July 1956, having a general overhaul as well as its rebuilding.

As referred to or the previous page, No 35014 is almost ready for a return to traffic. The presence of the lifting cables may indicate the engine had recently been reunited with its front bogie. (CR 105420ST)

The first of the Merchant Navy class to be rebuilt was No 35018 'British India Line', dealt with at Eastleigh between November 1955 and February 1956. Being the prototype modification there were some features unique to the engine, the most prominent being the dog-leg in the pipe run alongside the boiler. Notice too the lack of handrails on the smoke deflectors with just hand-holds provided. Hand rails were certainly fitted to all the type later - possibly their absence here may have been an immediate reaction to the Milton (Western Region) accident of 20 November 1955 when it was suggested the driver's view ahead may have been hampered by the presence of handrails on the deflectors of the Britannia class engine involved. The red coloured paint on the front axle of the bogie may also have been unique. (If the axles of other members of the type were so painted this was quickly covered over in workaday grime.) No 35018 is also shown with the then early BR tender motif whilst the handwheel controlling the steam supply to the manifold in the cab (at front of the firebox) may also be noted to be polished brass - later these handwheels were painted green. Why all the embellishments? Simply that No 35018, as the first of the type to be dealt with, was visiting Waterloo on Monday 13 February to be inspected in its new guise by Sir Brian Robertson and other members of the British Railways Board. Returning to Eastleigh the next day, it was soon rostered on revenue earning turns although not without some incident. Richard Derry and Iain Sixsmith report two failures in traffic before the end of the month. But these were teething troubles as No 35018 and her rebuilt sisters soon settled down to be reliable and more importantly, predictable. performers. Sadly such a gleaming appearance (and with the high running plate a definite family resemblance to the BR 'Britannia' class) was not maintained in traffic.
(CR 312040ST)

We now move on to the dynamometer car tests of No 35020 in its rebuilt state. The trials took place between Salisbury and Exeter in the early summer of 1956 (and return) involving the Churchward Dynamometer Car under the supervision of Mr S O Ell from Swindon. **Above** - The interior of the Dynamometer Car used with No 35020. (CR 109867ST) **Right -** At Exeter Central, where in June 1956, Mr Ell is posed in front of the engine. The original Bulleid tender was a temporary addition but was used as the high sides were better able to retain the necessary cables between the test car and the engine. No 35020 had also been the engine kept as a 'stand-by' during the 1948 exchange trials. (CR 105402ST)

The tests with No 35020 were intended to be a direct comparison with a member of the class in rebuilt form as against tests carried out with an original member, No 35022, which took place in 1953. Officially, the results showed a marked improvement, in the order of 20% increase in cylinder efficiency. But behind the scenes it was a slightly different story. No 35020 was in perfect ex-works condition and was operated so as to secure maximum efficiency. Three years earlier the original No 35022 had been literally thrashed, to such an extent that the result was bent coupling rods. Richard Derry and Ian Sixsmith also quote Eric Youldon when referring to a former Exmouth Junction Fireman. This time the story relates to the much vaunted improvement in coal consumption between the original and rebuilt engines, the man in question stating, "...we hardly noticed any difference."

Above - Quickly moving on to the rebuilding of the light Pacifics, No 34005 'Barnstaple' seen on one of its early appearances in rebuilt form, leaving Waterloo with a Bournemouth line service in the summer of 1957. A decade later the engine was no more, having been withdrawn at the end of 1966, it was cut up in 1967. Final mileage was in excess of 800,00 miles although more than half of this had been accrued in original form.
(CR312041ST)

Opposite - No 34032 appears less than elegant when being lifted at Eastleigh sometime in 1953. The front bogie will be seen to be missing although otherwise the engine appears complete, behind is No 35025. The engine record cards indicate the view must have been taken between 15-17 October, as this was the only time that year that both engines were present in the works together. No 34032 was in for a 'Light Causual' between 15 October and 14 November and with just the bogie removed would imply this was the start of the work. It was at the time an Exmouth Junction machine. No 35025 was similarly allocated and had been inside since 21 September receiving a 'Heavy Intermediate' whilst also having the safety valves re-set to 250psi.
(CR 3087955ST)

Pages 22/23 - Examples of work from the brass shop at Eastleigh, including 'Seaton' nameplate, squadron plates, class plate, a whistle and various other notices and gauges. The display had been arranged for a visit by a delegation from the Institute of Mechanical Engineers in 1955.
(CR 109882ST)

No 34003 'Plymouth' appearing like a model, brand-new from rebuilding in the late Summer of 1957. The engine had entered the works on 20 August, emerging in the form seen on 28 September including having received a general overhaul. Officially still allocated to Exmouth Junction this was changed to Bricklayers Arms from 8 October 1957, so after running in, the engine may well never have returned to Devon. Some idea of the limited life accrued by the type in their rebuilt form may be gauged from the 268,000 miles run between 1957 and withdrawal in September 1964. Beyond the fence line is the railway from Eastleigh to Fareham and after this the carriage sidings, Tipton yard and then the sidings associated with the carriage works. (CR BRS1040)

Black and White Interlude: 1

It must not be forgotten that 'SCT' took any number of b/w images: certainly colour was used more in later years but the earlier material is also well worth a view.

On 23 December 1949, for example, he recorded these two views of B4 No 30083 on the new extension then being constructed at Fawley Refinery. At the time No 30083 was an Eastleigh allocated engine and, apart from use on this inspection, may even have been on hire to the contractors.
(R Blencowe 38150)

BLACK and WHITE Interlude: 1

A refinery at Fawley had first been established in 1921 and initially remained operational until around 1939. For the duration of WW2 the site was used for storage of imported refined product. A major expansion was embarked upon in 1949 for which purpose some 1,200 acres of land were acquired. The new plant, primary distillation units, a catalytic cracker and numerous treating units were operational in 1951, the new facility officially opened on Friday 14 September 1951. In connection with this, a special train was run from Waterloo leaving at 8.27 am, non stop to Southampton Central arriving at 10.01 am. Here engines were changed in just six minutes, the main line locomotive not permitted on the branch, hence a pair of M7s was substituted. Arrival at Fawley was at 10.12am.

The return was at 3.25 pm from Fawley: Southampton Central from 4.57 to 5.04 pm and again non-stop to Waterloo arriving at 6.38 pm. Of note is the formation for the down run which consisted of 12 coaches including three restaurant cars. Somewhat puzzling is the formation for the return working stated to be '11 coaches' without further explanation.

In the view **opposite top**, M7s Nos 30242 and 30480 have charge of the return train complete with headboard on the approach to Southampton Central from Fawley.

Opposite bottom - No 34063 '229 Squadron' is ready to leave Southampton Central with the up working. (The engine was then allocated to Stewarts Lane but had just received a 'heavy intermediate' overhaul being released back to traffic just five days earlier.) (R Blencowe 38198A and 38198B)

Above - lightly earlier in the same year and unrelated to the above, S C Townroe recorded No 30850 'Lord Nelson' in Southampton Docks. Two of the men seen may not be identifiable, but the third standing on the tender is O S Nock. (R Blencowe 38197C)

Opposite page - In late October 1953, trials were undertaken with diesel shunter No 13014 as a possible steam replacement / supplement in Southampton Docks. No 13014 was one of five diesel shunters built at Derby in December 1952 and then allocated to Hither Green. On paper it was transferred (on loan) to Eastleigh week ended 1 November 1953 - and returned home again in the same period. From the limited time spent and the fact no further engine of the type was subsequently seen, we may conclude the trials were less than satisfactory but without further comment possible. (This engine survived to become BR No D3014 in 1957 and was withdrawn in 1973 and sold to the national Coal Board. It worked for its new owners in South Wales until 1989 when it was sold to the Paignton and Dartmouth Railway. It now carries the name 'Samson'.)
(R Blencowe 38221)

Above - US Army Transportation Corps shunter No 1952 at Eastleigh, probably around late 1946. The presence of the Bulleid tender in the background confirms the location. No 1952 was originally to have been SR No 64 but instead emerged as SR No 69, entering service with the Southern in November 1947. Behind is US Army No 1418 of Porter manufacture. This was one of five of the type which arrived at Eastleigh from the dump at Newbury and were subsequently returned. (The five were returned as the decision was made to standardise the engines made by the manufacturer Vulcan.) It was allocated SR No 63 but this was never carried. Ironically the five engines involved subsequently found use in (then) Yugoslavia. Minor external detail differences between the two types include the number of steps on the end of the side tank and rivet detail.

Right - An undated view of No 4326 which was at work in Southampton Docks from May 1946 onwards. This engine was to have been SR No 63 but instead would appear as SR No 74. Even so the SR number was never carried, the engine going straight through to BR days still with its USA livery. It subsequently became No 30074 in October 1948. In both cases the original small coal bunkers will be noted.
(R Blencowe 38077 and 38095A)

Opposite page - 'Government Sidings' Micheldever.

The 'Government Sidings' at Micheldever owe their origins to the development of Southampton Docks by the Southern Railway in the 1930s. Necessary reclamation along the foreshore west of the present Southampton Central station required thousands of tons of infill. To this end the cutting between the station and the tunnel at Micheldever was opened out and spoil transported the 17 miles to the required destination. In 1938 and no doubt in view of pending conflict, an oil storage depot was established built into what was the east side of the opened out cutting. SCT recorded these two views of the work at the time which also show the storage tanks in position ready for their 'concrete jacketing' to be attached. This concrete cover would later extend close to the same height as the actual cutting, almost 60 feet, and was intended to make the structure bomb-proof. The top of the bunker was also grassed over so as to be of little interest when seen from the air. (Perhaps the nearest this country came to the similarly heavily fortified U-boat pens built on the French Atlantic coast.) During WW2 the storage facility came into its own supplying various airfields with fuel. Later, in connection with D-Day, fuel from Micheldever was sent by pipeline direct to Southampton and thence across to Europe. (According to http://www.micheldevervillage.org.uk/archive_railway.html the Ministry of Defence has been unable to confirm or deny that PLUTO 'Pipe line under the ocean' actually ran alongside the railway track.

In 1943 17 sidings were added to the area between the oil depot and the main line, their purpose to provide an Ordnance Depot, which was manned by hundreds of military personnel. Post WW2, the sidings were used for stock storage, a situation that continued into the 1970s but eventually ceased as rolling stock rationalisation took effect. The oil terminal later reverted to civilian use, being used for bulk storage and distribution. One of the last occupants was Elf petroleum with operations eventually ceasing around March 1995. (R Blencowe 38026)

'T1' as SR No 2, at speed near Stoneham (south of Eastleigh). The date of the view cannot be confirmed, although it is likely to have been not long before the engine was withdrawn in February 1949 and so must therefore make this one of the last months of working. The train is almost certainly a Winchester Chesil - Southampton Terminus service (hence the GWR coach) as engine changing on services via the DNS line was still taking place at Winchester until as late as 1953. (R Blencowe 38170)

- and speaking of services from Winchester Chesil, upon takeover by the Southern Region of the line south of Newbury, SC Townroe made at least one footplate trip, no doubt to acquaint himself with this piece of railway that now came under his jurisdiction at Eastleigh so far as motive power was concerned. Here we see the result, from the cab of one of the batch of new BR Standard 4MT 2-6-0s then allocated to Eastleigh and intended as replacement for older Drummond 4-4-0s. The view was recorded in 1953 and is taken on Hockley (Shawford Junction) viaduct with the home signal cleared for the train to continue south towards Eastleigh. Sixty years later a signal of the type seen has been replaced on the viaduct which now no longer sees trains but is part of the national 'Sustrans' cycle network. (R Blencowe 38222)

Above - A rare view of the approach to Basingstoke from the cab of a 'Lord Nelson' pre 1939. This was one of a small series of very early colour views taken and is also the best. The train is signalled through platform 4. With the aid of his own biography, so many of the images within this book take on a new meaning and can be related to the various roles he held and tasks he was given. Could this one for example, be related to his involvement n the fitting of speed recorders to express engine types?
(CR 109869ST)

Right - Agreeably not of the best quality but historically very interesting. A 1952 view of an engineers / officers inspection service taking the west curve from Tunnel Junction (the signal box is in the background) Southampton, towards Southampton Terminus and Docks. Images of trains on this curve are extremely rare. Possibly a docks inspection working? No 30790 'Sir Villiars' is in charge.
(CR 312074ST)

The original 'Camelot'. 'N15' No 30742 built at Eastleigh in June 1919, the class was named by the Southern Railway post 1925. As BR No 30742, the engine lasted until February 1957 but the name would live on as it was subsequently carried by a BR Standard class 5, No 73082, the latter named in August 1959. In the view here the engine is seen at speed near Eastleigh in July 1953. (CR BRS1200)

In May 1952 SCT recorded 'H15' No 30476 near Dorchester in charge of a Weymouth to Nine Elms freight. A 'white-feather' can just be seen from the safety valves so presumably the engine was managing well on the climb from its starting point. No 30476 survived in traffic until the end of 1961. (CR 312045ST)

View from the driving trailer of the push-pull set operating the Ventnor West service on 18 May 1952. The train has just entered the 619 yard St Lawrence tunnel built with stone walls and a brick roof. The view is looking out of the east end of the tunnel with the train heading towards the terminus at Ventnor West. Services on the line from Merstone ceased from 15 September 1952. After track lifting the tunnel found a new use for a while growing mushrooms.
(CR 109866ST)

Opposite top - Watched by assembled throng, 'O2' No 32 'Bonchurch' in malachite green livery runs around its train (an RCTS special) in May 1952. The lines are: left to Sandown, right to Ventnor West.
(CR BRS828)

Opposite bottom - 'O2' No 14 'Fishbourne' taking water from the locomotive facility at the back of Brading station. The station signal box is visible behind the engine with the Ryde to Ventnor line out of sight but passing on the left. Diverging to the right in the distance was the branch to Bembridge.
(CR BRS826)

Above - The approach to Newport and Medina Bridge. At first glance their appears to be an issue with the second coach (S6365) comparing its angle relative to the first vehicle. But as the third vehicle is of similar profile and the crew are happily handing over the single line tablet all must be well. Unusually, apart from the date, May 1957, nothing else is recorded by SCT against this view.
(CR 109412)

This page bottom - - Cab view from an 'M7' tank heading down the 1 in 60 from Medstead towards Ropley on the Mid-Hants railway. Stephen Townroe took several views on this line on different occasions, often travelling on the footplate between his home at Farnham and Eastleigh. May 1957. (CR 109870ST)

Left - Approaching Winchester Junction with the signalman ready to receive the tablet for the section from Alresford. (SCT - private collection)

Opposite page - A final glimpse of railways of the Isle of Wight. 18 May 1953 sees 'E1' No W3 leaving Cowes with what is clearly marked as an RCTS special. CR 308797ST)

Left - Freight on the Meon Valley. Stephen Townroe's colour views on the Meon Valley line in east Hampshire taken around the time of closure in 1955 are well known and have been seen before. Indeed I well recall my reaction when he showed them to me at his home at Upham many years ago. The images on these pages though did not feature, probably, as I have since learnt, because they were taken before that time. (SCT was always very helpful but would never elaborate on a conversation or expand on the answer to a specific question. The impression gained was that he was disciplined and self controlled.) The train seen going away was recorded at Soberton, just south of Droxford and was hauled by a '700'. This was probably the daily up pick-up goods which, having shunted the yard at Wickham and possibly Mislingford siding, would then make its way north calling at Droxford, West Meon, Privett, East Tisted and finally Faringdon, en route to Alton.
(CR 109872ST)

Above - How the mighty have fallen. An unidentified 'T9' also near Soberton but this time in the down direction - were the views taken on the same day? The load appears to consist of at least a number of open wagons, probably coal with the next stop due at Wickham. In both cases the neatness of the permanent way will be noted with the bridge indicating the formation for a double line of rails which was never laid. The concrete pylons sunk into the ballast at intervals have a small metal insert set into the top. The distance from this to the outer rail will have been measured and will be rechecked at intervals to determine if 'creep' is taking place. Both of the views were taken in September 1953. In his book, 'Arthurs, Nelsons and Schools at work', SCT refers to an incident on the Meon Valley line when speaking of (general) staff issues. "Occasionally irregularities in working were reported by the public and one example had a sad ending. There were complaints of poaching on the MV line whilst examination of the signalbox records threw suspicion on a pick-up freight train and the length of time it had taken between two stations on certain days. An inspector then found a train stopped and unattended in mid-section, and on blowing the whistle the driver, fireman and guard came out of the woods, with rabbit nets. The case was still *sub-judice* when the driver took his own life. Rabbits on railway embankments were considered fair game for railway staff."
(CR 312063ST)

'M7' No 30035 on a down 'pull-push' working approaching Corfe Castle on the Swanage branch in 1956. Oh if the A351 were so quiet today!
(CR 308796ST)

Opposite page, contrasts at Swanage. **Top** - In 1938 LMS '2P' No 628 was recorded on the turntable at Swanage with train identification No M811 shown. What this service was, is not reported but presumably an excursion via the Somerset & Dorset line with the engine being made ready for the return working. The engine carries a '22A' shedplate for Bristol Barrow Road. In the background is 'T9' No 713.
(R Blencowe 38034)

Bottom - Nineteen years later in 1957, the engine is now an unidentified BR Standard 4MT 2-6-0, already turned and being prepared ready for a northbound service. Alongside the pile of ashes has grown somewhat over the years.
(CR 109875ST)

Above - With a backdrop of Southampton Docks, another 'M7', this time No 30127 traverses Redbridge causeway with a Fawley to Southampton passenger service in 1954.
(CR 312052ST)

Above - Cranleigh on the branch between Guildford and Christ's Hospital. SCT reported this view as '...changing staffs with military precision...' . It would hardly be fair to suggest the performance was simply due to his presence, as the importance of ensuring the correct staff was carried (and not 'over-carried') was a time-honoured and regular feature of single line operation. The image was no doubt taken on one of his regular trips to and from the works at Brighton. August 1954.
(CR BRS1113)

Opposite page - One year later in 1955, Stephen Townroe recorded two trains crossing at the station and then one departing north towards Guildford. The yard appears noticeably devoid of traffic whilst the signalman may have been a little too eager in replacing the starting signal as this should have remained at 'off' until the departing train had passed clear of all points and crossings locked by that lever. The station here was situated in the delightful sounding Hogspudding Lane. The line through Cranleigh closed on 14 June 1965.
(CR 109883ST and 109884ST)

Above - On 19 April 1956 a trial took place of a 300-ton coal train between Horsham and Guildford and return. Motive power was a diesel-electric shunting engine No 13219. Special attention was paid as to the ability to start and stop on various gradients. If satisfactory, the intention was to diagram such motive power for ordinary freight trains over the branch later in the year. Clearly, loaded coal wagons were used to make up the load with the view taken either from a guard's van or possibly even the cab of the locomotive. The train has just left Baynards and is heading south towards Baynards Tunnel and Rudgwick.
(CR 109880ST)

Opposite - No prizes for identifying the Hayling Island branch. There are of course numerous views of the line in the 1960s, but this one is a decade earlier on 23 July 1952 when 'AIX' No 32661 was recorded shortly after having left Havant on the way to the terminus.
(CR un-numbered)

This page and opposite top - In 1956 the BBC set up to record the sound of the 'Golden Arrow' passing through Paddock Wood at speed. Why exactly this particular sound and / or location were required was not specified so we are left to muse on a news item or one for a radio programme. (The latter would perhaps be unlikely as surely there would have been numerous sounds of steam trains in the archives at Broadcasting House.) Whatever, the equipment was duly set up and the BBC went to work - with numerous technicians! Here we see the actual train - one take only would have been possible - and the BBC transport. What exactly SCT's role was in the proceedings is equally mysterious as he was by then already well-ensconced at Eastleigh and out of the area.
(CR 312057ST and 109879ST)

THE BBC

Right - Reported as also taken in 1956, so presumably at the same time, was this view of 'Schools' No 30926 'Repton' is approaching Paddock Wood with a Folkestone to Charing Cross working. (CR 312058ST)

Above - Exmouth Junction shed in April 1957. Centre stage is 'N' No 31842 replete with 'Meldon dust' - the brown covering adhering to the front of the cylinders and bottom of the firebox. At least five other Bulleids can be seen whilst on the extreme left of the depot the tall section is what was known locally as the 'Catherderal' (lifting shop), so called because of its cavernous interior.
(CR 312054ST)

Opposite page - Two hundred and twenty miles east we see the modern depot at Ashford, dating from 1931 and which was for the most part often heavily congested with steam power. The similarity in design with Exmouth Junction will also be noted. In this 1956 view a 'Mogul' and a member of the 'C' class are parallel with each other as they reach the shed entry / exit.
(CR 109878ST)

Opposite top - 'C2X' No 32553 on the turntable at Bricklayers Arms in May 1956. This engine was then allocated to Three Bridges and survived in service until August 1961. It was reduced to scrap at Ashford just one month later.
(CR 308802ST)

Opposite bottom - Dorchester shed in May 1952, the location of Stephen Townroe's first appointment as 'Depot Foreman' in 1938. Views of the shed in black and white are rare (but see above) - colour rarer still. Visible are three members of the 'O2' 0-4-4T type, plus No 30743 'Lyonnesse' and an unidentified Drummond 'H15' 4-6-0 in the background. (With apologies for deterioration of the image as witness the fain horizontal blue line towards the base of the view.)
(CR BRS 441)

Above - Dorchester shed in 1938, probably as seen by Stephen Townroe when he was first appointed here. Compared with the view on the previous page the only major structural difference appears to be cladding which was added to the front of the timber 1875 extension some time after this photograph was taken. It may be noted that the locomotives seen face east - back towards Bournemouth and Southampton. Whilst SR engines did indeed work to and from Weymouth, there was a charge levied for use of the GWR turntable at what was then the GWR shed at Weymouth. Hence for economy purposes tender-first working when running light was the norm south of Dorchester even if this may not always have been the choice of the footplate crew. (As an example see the lower view on p2.) The shed allocation was maintained up until the time of regional boundary changes in April 1950, after which, with Weymouth now coming under the control of the Southern Region, the importance of the shed diminished, although it did not finally succumb until the summer of 1957.
(R Blencowe 38031)

Left and opposite bottom - Views of Bournemouth shed (and station) from the height of the roof over the lifting road. On the left 'L11' No 158 is moving on the road alongside the lifting area and in the bottom view is seen on one of the roads leading from the turntable. The gap in the roof of the lifting road was to allow clearance height for the sheer-legs. Whilst some degree of protection was afforded to the fitters in this area it will also be noted that it was totally open on one side. Again in the view opposite bottom, we see a view of the coaling area - Bournemouth always was cramped - note the view may show the new 65' turntable, installed in 1938. (R Blencowe 38025 and 38025A)

Opposite top - 'Schools' No 914 'Eastbourne' in gleaming condition at Bournemouth in 1938 recently released from Eastleigh works with Lemaitre blastpipe and wide chimney. Fitters Alf Saunders and Cecil Knott are about to open the smokebox door. (R Blencowe 38030)

Above - Twelve years later and the scene at Bournemouth reveals two gleaming 'S15's now in BR livery, another 4-6-0 and an LMS 4-4-0. The latter was clearly off the Somerset & Dorset but perhaps slightly unusually was being dealt with here rather than at nearby Branksome depot. In the background may just be seen the tower of the water softener, brought into use in 1938. Bournemouth depot also features in another memory from the 'Arthurs Nelsons and Schools at work' volume, "In the maintenance of 'Arthurs' no depot could rival Bournemouth in the 1930s when the inimitable Joe Elliott had charge there. Joe, who had started life as a fitter, contended that Eastleigh Works did not fit axleboxes properly and whenever a newly repaired 'Arthur' arrived, he had it put under the hoist for the axleboxes to be made a tighter fit. The process would be repeated as and when a driver reported axlebox knock, so that Bournemouth 'Arthurs' had a reputation for sweet running. To ensure his 'Arthurs' would run the 111 miles from Waterloo to Bournemouth West with an ample margin of water in the 5,000 gallon tenders, Joe would renew the piston rings frequently; in fact he reckoned that his methods of maintenance rendered superfluous the compilation of mileage records. The day came when, in connection with some mishap in the London area, he was instructed to send to Waterloo the complete records of one of his engines, for the information of a Ministry of Transport inspector. After some delay, the records were produced, all written in fresh ink. Suspicions being aroused, a few days later a high official arrived at Bournemouth without warning, demanding to see all the other records, after which it was Joe who was sent to Waterloo for a dressing-down."
(R Blencowe 38169)

Opposite - 'T9' No 337 on the turntable at Yeovil Junction in July 1939. We know that by 1938 SCT was ensconced at Dorchester but clearly he also travelled around (work or 'pleasure' is not reported) whilst it would seem there were also a number of views of locomotives on turntables in the collection. Was this even a 'project' he had been involved in? The '2314' code is not explained unless this was the code for a possible 'trial' evacuation train?
(R Blencowe 38039)

We know little of the two views seen here (both also having the same reference number as that on the previous page) other than they depict 'U' No 1628 and again reported as the turntable at Yeovil in July 1939. Clearly manual labour was called for here, the additional muscle in the form of the 'bowler hat' an interesting consideration. The weight being moved was in excess of 100 tons with the whole ensemble just fitting neatly on to the turntable. One slightly unrelated comment from SCT - but connected at least by reference to the West of England main line, concerns a note from SCT over the various cats that were 'allocated' to each depot. "...office cats, stores cats and the half-wild ones in coal stacks. Harold Attwell, one of Maunsell's testing staff, recalled that a cat walked out of the coal when an 'Arthur' was passing Woking on a Waterloo - Salisbury express. 'Pussy', presumably a Nine Elms resident, was consequently 're-allocated' to Salisbury shed".
(R Blencowe 38039)

Opposite top - Bricklayers Arms in 1944 (SCT obviously still had access to film for his camera), with 'Schools' No 934 'St Lawrence' and 'WD' 2-8-0 No 7422 visible. No 934 was the engine that had borne the brunt of the 11/12 May 1941 wartime attack whilst standing on Cannon Street bridge but was repaired and is seen here seemingly in green rather than all-over black. The cab side window however will be noted to be plated over. Notice also the tarpaulin draped from the cab roof. The following year No 934 was repainted overall black but reverted to malachite green again in 1946.
(R Blencowe 38054A)

Opposite bottom - No 901 'Winchester' seen in 1941 still in SR green but with the cab side window removed. The location is the turntable at Ewer Street. The facilities, turntable, water tower and coaling stage here, were adjacent to Southwark Park (goods) and remained in use until 1961.
(R Blencowe 38008)

Above - '72C' Yeovil Town depot in March 1957 with SR locomotives dominant. To the right the former cottage doubled as the mess room and also the shed foreman's office. The view was taken from Dodham Bridge with Dodham brook just visible on the extreme right. Notwithstanding the limited life anticipated for steam, major expenditure came in 1959 in consequence of the closure of the shed at Yeovil Pen Mill. This was in the form of a tall water tank erected at the rear of the shed. Beyond the station the line splits, left to Yeovil Pen Mill and eventually Castle Cary, and right to Yeovil Junction or south to Dorchester and Weymouth.
(CR109874ST)

Pages 66/67 - 'D3' 0-4-4T No 32390, formerly 'St Leonards', on the turntable a Horsham in August 1954. This was the last member of the D3/D3X class to remain in service, outliving its compatriots by more than two years. Although not the one reported to have accrued the highest mileage, it still achieved 1.4 million in a 65-year life. In the summer of 1954 No 32390 was mainly rostered on Brighton to Horsham workings or else acted as station/ shed pilot at Brighton. Despite several close-calls, any of which might have led to withdrawal, it was finally summoned to Ashford for breaking in the autumn of 1955 but due to a labour shortage was towed to Brighton and finally succumbed at the end of November. (CR BRS298)

SCT took at least two colour views of the line up at Eastleigh during the devastating locomen's strike. Lasting two weeks from 29 May to 14 June 1955, the point at issue was pay differentials - amounting to what was in effect the then price of a packet of cigarettes. The strike was called just days after Conservative Anthony Eden had secured a victory in the General Election. With commerce still totally dependent upon the railways, the government was forced into a climb down and the British Transport Commission settled the pay claim. Whilst drivers received their demand, their mates on the footplate, the firemen, felt they had done less well. The longer lasting effect was a change of government policy so as to be less dependent upon rail transport. (CR 109886ST)

Above - A grimy 'T9' 4-4-0, as BR No 30714 on the road leading up to the coaling stage at Eastleigh in 1948. Whilst the locomotive has been renumbered on the smokebox and cab, it is worth noting the Southern 'sunshine' lettering that still exists on the tender. Whether the engine was especially posed, (SCT would certainly have the authority to request it), or it had genuinely been used to shunt the ramp of the coaling stage is not certain. (CR BRS1025)

Right - The 'Royal' engine, 'T9' No 30119 - well the one that was usually kept pristine for special workings. It is seen here in spotless guise at Eastleigh in 1948, probably just after a works visit of 8 April to 1 May, when it was also repainted. During WW2 No 119 had been kept under a sheet at Nine Elms for some time but latterly was pressed into ordinary service. Why it achieved such regular status is not reported, but it was also not enough to ensure its survival as it was withdrawn in 1952 and scrapped the following year. (R Blencowe 38120)

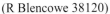

On 16 November 1955, whilst in charge of the 9.00 am ex-Waterloo, No 35016 'Elders Fyffes' failed at Gillingham with fractures to all coupling rods and on subsequent examination, cracking to the axleboxes. The known failure of the crank axle on sister engine No 35020 is of course well reported, but what may not be known so widespread is that in 1954 No 35023 broke a tender axle near Broad Clyst whilst No 35025 broke a coupling rod at Honiton in the same year. Here Townroe's views show the components of No 35016 subsequent to the mishap (unfortunately not the engine). Even so the Gillingham incident does not seem to have prompted any immediate response and we are left then to ponder over the initial cause and subsequent effect.
(CR 105423ST and CR109881ST)

Bournemouth in 1939 with what is reported as a failed hornguide - we are not told the locomotive concerned nor the name of the individual - but do refer to the caption on p52. (CR109871ST)

Aside from the books he was involved with, Stephen Townroe also penned a number of articles in the 'Meccano Magazine' on railway topics. Naturally these were written in such a way as to appeal to the age group of the readership and appeared either under his own name or under the pseudonym 'Shed Superintendent '. The following appeared in the issue for April 1956 under the heading, 'Whistle Language':

"To the enthusiast the delights of railway observation are not limited by what he sees. The hiss of a brake valve, the 'chink' of buffers or the call of a whistle - all these sounds convey information to him, even during darkness or in the compartment of a train.

The whistle language is an interesting study. The use of the whistle in certain circumstances is, of course, laid down strictly in the Rulebook in force on all the main line companies. To take examples, there is the long full note used when a train is approaching an adverse signal, to remind the signalman of the presence of the train, usually followed by the 'pop' whistle when the signal is cleared. Drivers of freight trains must give three or more short, sharp whistles if the assistance of the guard's hand brake is required and if a banking engine is in rear, crow or 'cock-a-doodle-oo' whistles are exchanged between the drivers before starting the train whether freight or passenger.

A series of pop whistles is required by the Rules to be sounded frequently when a train is travelling on the wrong line in an emergency or in special circumstances making this working necessary. It is interesting to note that the use of a succession of pop whistles has become the accepted warning of sudden danger by reason of the agitated sound of this call. If, for example, six or more hurried whistles are heard in a shunting yard it may mean a driver has spotted a wagon running away or observed a shunter walking into danger. This has saved many lives, and on hearing it you will notice that railwaymen at once look round, to see what is wrong.

Local whistle codes may be listed in the Appendix to the Rules issued by each company, or in the Divisional Instructions, which require certain whistle calls to be used at junctions to denote to the signalman the correct route of the train or the destination of a light engine. The understanding of these codes requires some local knowledge. There are nearly always descriptive code whistles in force at the exit from a locomotive depot, especially at a big depot whence light engines travel to a number of different places to take up their duties.

Then there are variants in whistle calls used by individual drivers. For instance the Rules stipulate whistling during the passage of long tunnels but the type of whistle is not defined in words, and I could always tell when a certain driver was in charge of the train by hearing his peculiar and effective tunnel whistle, which was a long drawn-out wail ending in an expressive 'pip'.

Other whistle calls established by custom, which certainly do not appear in the Rulebook, include the 'Cooee' whistle used in greeting one's colleagues on the line, the V-sign whistle according to Mr Churchill, and the jubilant whistling that occurs to celebrate the return home of a football team that has won the Cup Final. Last there is the short, low whistle, known to schoolboys as the 'Cave' warning, which on the railway means simply, 'Look out, here comes the Superintendent.'"

'700' class 0-6-0 No 30339 looking decidedly worse for wear at Eastleigh in February 1953. We are not told of the circumstances but evidently it was not considered terminal as the engine was repaired and lasted in service until the early 1960s. (CR 312062ST)

Sometime around 5.00 am on Tuesday 18 September 1962, No 30770 'Sir Piranius' (sometimes spelt 'Prianius), had charge of the 2.30 am newspaper train from Waterloo. The train was scheduled to take an hour to reach Basingstoke where the front portion was taken on to Southampton and eventually Bournemouth. The rear five vehicles all BR Mk1 vans, were taken on to Winchester and Eastleigh, the eventual destination for the train being Portsmouth although some of the newspapers were intended to continue on to the Isle of Wight. Departure from Eastleigh was scheduled for 4.38 am, although here (but unknown at the time), would be the last scheduled stop the train actually made. Shortly afterwards it had come to a halt near Botley with a fire on board the first vehicle which rapidly spread though the van fuelled by the volume of consumables on board. How long the train remained disabled is not reported, although we know the first

emergency call was not received until 5.33 am, by which time most of the train was well alight. It appears there was some confusion over the location given to the emergency services with the result that four of the five vehicles were destroyed although the fifth, containing mails, was satisfactorily detached. There were no reports of injury. Subsequent investigation failed to confirm the cause although suspicion fell in two areas, firstly the fact that when the train had separated at Basingstoke a blank had not been fitted to the corridor connection of the first coach and it was felt a spark from the engine may have lodged in this area. The alternative was a carelessly discarded cigarette which smouldered and eventually generated enough heat to set alight debris on the floor. (See also article in 'Southern Way Preview'.) (Above - CR 312071ST, right SC T private collection.)

(Pages 74 to 77) On 31 January 1956, 'H15' No 30477 was working the 11.30 pm freight to Eastleigh when it ran through the stop-blocks at the end of the down shunting neck immediately prior to Fishbourne Crossing, continuing on through a hedge to end up at a somewhat drunken angle within a private garden. The Fratton breakdown attended and after the drawbar between engine and tender had been disconnected, this latter item was successfully pulled back on to the rails. An initial attempt was made to recover No 30477 in similar fashion but the engine had literally 'gone to ground' so proving rather more elusive. It was to be a further two weeks before a successful attempt was made using block-and-tackle. No 30477 was then hauled away to Eastleigh for inspection and repair*, although destined to remain in revenue earning service until 1959. The views were all taken on 1 February 1956, indicating there was much activity within the first 24 hours, although clearly this initial attempt at recovery was unsuccessful .
(CR 109854ST and 312067ST to 312070ST)

* The records indicate the engine was in Eastleigh Works from 24 February to 8 March 1956, although as indicated above, if the engine was recovered around 14 February it was clearly some days before it was officially accepted for repair.

We see here a good indication of how No 30477 was hauled back on to the rails. Firstly the chains around the boiler were used to stabilise the engine after which sleepers were placed underneath with the engine jacked sufficiently to allow rails to be laid. The flanges were then set into the rails allowing it to be hauled back to the railway proper. Townroe had used a similar method to re-rail the 'Lord Nelson' that went down the back at Shawford in 1952 and his expertise in this way was again called upon for the derailment of the 'Battle of Britain' 'Spitfire' at Hither Green some years later. (See 'Southern Way Special No 8'.) Notice the boiler handrails have been cut through on No 30477. (This method of re-railing with rails tied to the wheels of an overturned locomotive is believed to have been devised by SCT and was subsequently used throughout the BR system.

Above - Incident at Reading South in June 1954. Watched no doubt by passengers passing trains on the WR main line, 'S15' No 30834 is gently lifted back on to the rails. Nothing specific is known of the incident although as it is in steam we may surmise the engine had derailed whilst manoeuvring at slow speed. The crane is probably from Guildford and it will be noted that its chimney has not been swung vertical - see also page 99. (CR 312072ST)

Opposite page - Reported as 'derailed petrol tankers' at Salisbury in 1968. No information has been found on the incident itself although Townroe's caption for the lower view is somewhat startling, "Catching petrol leaking from tank". Modern day 'Health and Safety' officers may take note. (CR109858ST and CR109859ST)

In May 1960 diesel-shunter No 15231 failed to stop at the buffers when engaged in shunting in the yards at Eastleigh. Damage to the engine itself would appear to have been minimal although buffer-lock ensued involving at least the first vehicle. Here the recalcitrant machine and first wagon are seen temporarily immobile but shortly to be rescued by steam.

(CR109857ST, CR109858ST and CR109888ST)

Above - Strawberry Hill EMU depot in June 1955. Suburban unit No 4318 has well and truly managed to close operations around the depot having jumped a crossover during shunting operations. Again steam has come to the rescue in the shape of the crane plus an 'M7' and '700'.
(CR 109889ST)

Opposite top - 'E3' 0-6-2T No 32167 has the indignity of having been deliberately derailed at Stewarts Lane in 1955 for the purpose of testing German hydraulic jacks and lifting equipment. This must have been one of the final tasks set for the engine as it was withdrawn in the same year.
(CR109861ST)

Opposite bottom - A further re-railing test but this time some years later in 1970. An inflatable air jack is being used to raise the wagon concerned. The location is not given.
(CR 109860ST)

Not an accident as such, instead we see 'C2X' No 32437 at Brighton in 1956 temporarily minus its rearmost set of wheels. The engine and tender are in smart plain black livery with the engine part certainly 'down at the back end' as witness the disparity in height between the running plate of engine and tender. No 32437 survived in traffic until 1959. (CR 312055ST)

Above - 'WC' No 34043 displaying definite evidence of pyrotechnics sometime in 1951. The circumstances are not reported although there is a suggestion that the incident may have occurred on the Somerset & Dorset line.
(CR 312042ST)

Right - May 1948 and another Bulleid in trouble. This time it is No 21C119 'Bideford', at the time running as an oil-burner (notice the oil tank in the coal space). This was one of two 'Light Pacifics' converted to burn oil (the other was No 21C136). 'Bideford' was converted between June and July 1947 but was refitted to burn coal in August/ September 1948. The damaged casing will be noted not to be in the area of the firebox and in consequence we may assume this was another example of oil from the bath leaking into the lagging under the casing and having being set alight by sparks from the brake blocks.
(R Blencowe 38096A)

DIESEL DAYS

Above - The fuelling point at Waterloo for the main line diesels - open air and gravity fed from a strategically placed rail tank in the sidings on the east side of the station. LMS design No 10000 is having its tanks topped up. (CR DE 1727)

Left - Sister engine, No 10001, at Southampton central with an up Waterloo express in 1953. This was the lead image used to accompany the article quoted on the next page.
(R Blencowe 38212A)

Opposite page - Around the same time, No 10000 was recorded on the 'Bournemouth Belle' passing Woodfidley in the New Forest.
(CR 232374ST)

Another, slightly earlier Townroe article, appeared in the 'Meccano Magazine' for August 1953. Entitled 'Diesel twins Fight it Out', it started by referring to a piece in the July 1952 issue when a run behind No 10201 on the 'Royal Wessex' was reported. This time the subject was the work of Nos 10000/1 on the Southern Region with the initial comment that, "The Southern diesels hold enough fuel to run to Exeter twice; but the Midland diesels require re-fuelling between trips and their water supply must be replenished under pressure through underframe connections, whereas the Southern diesels can take water from an ordinary water column. The Midland diesels therefore require slightly longer marginal time between trips." Townroe went on to describe how, "... that notwithstanding their nominal power rating being slightly less than the SR machines, their performance closely approached that of their more modern rivals, but just how closely still remained to be seen when on 23 April 1953, No 10000 backed on to the 448-ton train forming the down 'Royal Wessex' at Waterloo for the first time.

"The 'Wessex' timing of 55 minutes to pass Worting Junc., 55¼ miles from Waterloo, is considered to be a tougher proposition than the 51 minutes allowed for the accelerated 'Atlantic Coast Express' normally loaded to 365 tons. The Southern twins had shown that they could achieve a time of 51 minutes to Worting Junc. with the 'Royal Wessex'. How much under the 55 minute allowance could the Midland diesel No 1000 achieve with the same train?

"On the day of the trip, weather conditions were good; there was a nice dry rail and no head wind. Driver E Lane of Bournemouth was in charge; he sat high up in the American-style nose-end of No 10000 waiting for the guard to give him the green flag. The big 16-cylinder engine was ticking over steadily, but the noise in the engine room prevents conversation, and passage through the interior of the Midland diesels is not very easy, as they are more cramped for space than the Southern design.

"Promptly at 4.35pm we made an excellent start, assisted by a vigorous push from the Drummond M7 tank engine at the rear, an engine, incidentally, that was 50 years older than the train engine. Over Westminster Bridge Road the driver put the control handle of the diesel to full power and we roared along through Vauxhall, past Queens Road and reached Clapham Junction in six minutes, one minute less than schedule. There the 40 mph speed restriction was carefully observed and then full power was restored, but between Raynes Park and Malden the signals ahead could be seen showing double-yellow and then single-yellow, and in the distance a red light. We were clearly on the tail of an electric train that would get out of our way at Surbiton, so power had to be shut off and we coasted at 50 mph., watching the signals turn to green as we approached them. Just before Surbiton, Driver Lane was able to open the throttle wide again, and Hampton Court Junction was passed in 15 seconds less than the 18 minutes allowed.

continued overleaf/-

2000hp SR diesel-electric No 10203 passing Woking with the WR dynamometer car sometime between 28 June and 1 July 1953. The results of these and subsequent tests without the dynamometer car, showed this engine was 'a coach' better than its smaller-engined sisters. 2000hp thus showed the way forward as regards main-line traction and in turn led directly to the English Electric type 4, later class 40. (See: *'Southern Way Special Issue No 1: 10201-3 on the Southern'* - out of print in 2014 although copies may still be available through second hand sources.)
(CR 221778ST)

continued from previous page:-

"For the subsequent 37 miles to Worting Junc., No 10000 was kept at maximum output, without any adverse signals. Woking Junction was the next timing point, due to be passed in 28 minutes for the 24¾ miles. We did it in 27 minutes 30 seconds, and it certainly looked as if we could keep on the right side of the schedule but only by a small margin. It was not until we had passed Farnborough that the speedometer settled above the 60 mark. Through Fleet and Winchfield we maintained a steady 65-68 mph, and passing Basingstoke we found we had 2½ miles to go and over four minutes in which to do it. Eventually we clocked 53 minutes at Worting, two minutes to the good. If we had not been checked by that electric train, we might have been three minutes to the good, but obviously could not achieve a 51-minute timing, like the Southern diesels. However, there was not much in it!

"On this showing, it was evident that the Midland diesels can handle the same trains as the Southern diesels, but that if it became necessary to recover lost time caused by track relaying or traffic congestion, then the Southern twins would probably show up some superiority. The contest continues!

"With the present tendency to tighten up the schedules of the principal passenger trains, the recovery of time needs greater effort than before. Consequently even a small reserve of power in the locomotive is most valuable to a keen driver."

Preparing the engine for the 'Devon Belle', 'Merchant Navy' No 21C18 'British India Line' at Salisbury in 1948. The front and side train nameboards were painted red with yellow lettering. Introduced in June 1947, the service had only been running a few months when on 22 September 1947 one of the side wingplates detached itself from the engine as the up and down services passed each other between Sidmouth Junction and Honiton. Several windows were broken on the down service and a number of passengers injured. (See article on the 'Devon Belle' in 'Southern Way No 2'.)
(R Blencowe 38088 and 38088A)

Somerset & Dorset Memories

Opposite top - Petrol driven inspection trolley near Blandford sometime in 1940. (R Blencowe 38041B)

Opposite bottom - Signalman Tom Mobb with the station bell at Edington Junction, March 1952. The lettering is 'SCR 1862' Opened as 'Edington Road in 1856' it was renamed as seen in 1890 but in 1953 became Edington Burtle consequent upon the closure of the branch to Bridgwater. (R Blencowe 38202B)

This page - Checking the alignment and setting of the tablet catcher on No 53802 at Midford in 1951. (R Blencowe38187 and 38187A)

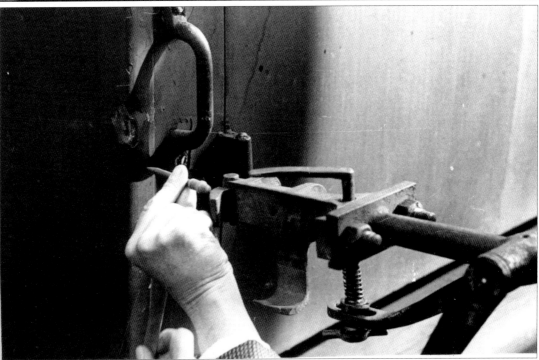

In July 1939 'SCT' took a footplate trip over the Somerset & Dorset line north from Bournemouth. Here we have the view as his train passes Shepton Mallet with an LMS '2P' piloting a 'Black 5'. (R Blencowe 38038)

Royal working (empty stock) at Fareham in July 1952. The details are not given although it is believed a shunt move was also involved as 'T9' No 30282 is also referred to on the same occasion. Aside from the polished buffers, the special white vacuum and steam pipes will be noted.
(R Blencowe 38209)

'LN' No 30853 'Sir Richard Grenville' slowly moving off-shed at Eastleigh in the late summer of 1948. Townroe comments, '...this was the first member of the class to be allocated to Eastleigh...', although eventually all 16 would find their way to the depot. This concentration was Townroe's own idea, his thought being that the men would thus become used to the class which, whilst lacking the occasional brilliance of a Bullied, were far more dependable and therefore predictable.
(R Blencowe 38178)

Opposite - No 21C110, later given the name 'Sidmouth', completed at Brighton in September 1945 and seen here on the turntable at Redhill on 31 October of the same year.

Right - The same engine, this time either having just arrived (or being made ready to leave) on the same date.

(R Blencowe 38058 and 38058A)

Driver Fred Scott with his regular engine, 'King Arthur' No 30783 'Sir Gillemere' at Eastleigh on 23 December 1949. The 'ELGH' initials will be noted on the buffer beam, a short lived exercise which would soon be replaced with a conventional shed code/letter as per LMS practice.
(R Blencowe 38153)

Locomotives and Lineside

Britannia's on the Southern.

Left - Clearly a Locomotive Inspector, although regretfully the name is not given, alongside No 70009 'Alfred the Great' depicted at Bournemouth West whilst working the 'Bournemouth Belle' duty. The engine was then almost brand new, having only entered traffic in May 1951.
(R Blencowe 38196)

Above - According to the slide listing, this view was taken in July 1957 and shows No 70014 'Iron Duke' at Branksome depot (Bournemouth) having been turned and waiting to reverse back to Bournemouth West station. The line on the right is one side of the triangle taking trains to and from Bournemouth Central.
(CR 312076ST)

Left - A pristine No s21C116 'Bodmin' at Eastleigh in 1948. Southern 'sunshine' lettering and three yellow stripes are set off with the temporary 's' prefix to the original Southern number and with 'British Railways' on the tender. Interesting that the circular brass disc remains on the smokebox.
(CR BRS424)

Above - No 34009 'Lyme Regis' with the breakdown crane either just before or subsequent to the view seen on p78. The headcode is interesting and relates just to breakdown trains, unusually also for the SR being non route-specific. The same code in the form of a 'V' was also carried by No 34051 when hauling the funeral train for Winston Churchill in 1965.
(CR 312043ST)

Next page - Possibly one of the last views taken of 'H2' No 32424 'Beachy Head' in immaculate external condition at Eastleigh in 1958. 'West Country' No 34006 'Bude' is behind. We would be forgiven for believing the 'Atlantic' was ex-works but sadly the reverse was the case as the engine was withdrawn in April. Eric Best from Winchester was employed to cut-up withdrawn engines at the back of the works at that time. He recalls, "The engine came round to us and we ignored it for as long as possible hoping someone would come up with a plan to save her - there was certainly a rumour going around that she would be spared. If anyone asked, we would remove something non-essential but in the end there was no choice….".
(CR BRS359)

Above - Another breakdown train view, double headed by 'K' No 32338 and an unidentified member of the 'N' class. The slide was taken at Tonbridge in May 1956. Double heading a breakdown train was not unusual and would usually take place if a replacement engine were needed to take over from a disabled loco. In this way there was a saving on line-occupancy.
(CR 312056ST)

Opposite top - A slightly puzzling image in two ways. Firstly 'C' class No 31712, seen here at Brighton in February 1956, is certainly in steam with what are possibly the footplate crew in the background. Townroe's caption however refers to 'splitting engine and tender'. Does this mean a defect had been found? The other point of interest is the position of the front vacuum pipe. This has been re-arranged from its usual mounting next to the coupling and now stands alongside the buffer. A similar puzzle is the pipework and bracket at the opposite buffer and which is not associated with de-icing gear fitted to ten members of the class. (Upon withdrawal in February 1957, the tender shown, No 2964, was modified for service with the weed-killing train and renumbered DS1473.)
(CR 312059ST)

Opposite bottom - 'L' class 4-4-0 No 31760 seemingly being prepared for the road at Tonbridge in May 1956.
(CR 312046ST)

Overleaf - A 'King Arthur' in its later years but still looking very much up to standard. No 30448 'Sir Tristram' at Exmouth Junction in April 1957. The engine was then 22 years old and would be just 25 when it was withdrawn in 1960. Behind is No 35014 'Nederland Line'. No 30448 carries a Salisbury '72B' shedplate.
(CR BRS385)

Opposite - A stunning portrayal of 'T9' No 30719 with an officer's inspection train at Woking in 1955. Clearly SCT was 'in the know' on a number of occasions, being present to record the unusual. Aside from the 'West of England' headcode nothing else is mentioned about the working.
(CR 312047ST)

Above - Standard 'Class 5' No 73080 running on the down fast line just past Shawford and passing under Bowker's footbridge - Mary and Judi Townroe are seen waving to the train. This was a private bridge leading from 'Colleton' - the then Townroe family residence - on to Shawford Down. In the background the two home signals guard the up fast and up relief lines, the two converging just out of camera. It was here in July 1952 that 'Howard of Effingham' came to grief in consequence of the driver misreading the signal seen and believing he was actually on the fast line. Living so close, Townroe was rapidly on the scene. (See also p109). Bowkers footbridge was so named as it had once connected two residences belonging to the Bowker family - one either side of the line. It was to the house on the west side that the Townroe family moved in 1958. (In the early years of the 20th century Alfred Bowker had been responsible for the setting up of the stone on which Winchester's renowned King Alfred's statue now stands in Winchester Broadway.)
(CR 312044ST)

Opposite - No 34006 'Bude' running well through Weybridge with the 3.00 pm Waterloo to Exeter service in the summer of 1955. The engine has its characteristic long smoke-deflectors whilst the train is formed of modern BR Mk1 vehicles.
(BRS 1097)

Above - From ground level, the approach to Shawford station from the south. What is an original 'Merchant Navy' is running on the up fast line and has passed the up line signals referred to in the view on p107. The up relief, on the left, will end very shortly - its sand-drag just visible in the distance.
(CR 109853ST)

Above - Old and new at Eastleigh in August 1962. 'Drummond 'M7' No 30053 is alongside Riddles '9F' No 92211, the latter almost pristine safe for evidence of a leak from the regulator valve. The 'M7' type was long associated with Eastleigh although their work and in consequence their numbers had diminished significantly since the introduction of the Hampshire DEMU scheme from 1957. No 30053 was destined to be one of the lucky ones and was saved for posterity. Eastleigh played host to a number of '9F's in the early 1960s, both visiting and also allocated to the depot for use on northbound oil trains from Fawley.
(BRS 1059)

Opposite top - August 1953, and an unidentified but no doubt almost new 76xxx 2-6-0 is coasting around the curve with a train from the Romsey direction heading towards Southampton. The Western Region stock would indicate this was probably a Cardiff or Bristol service possibly destined for Portsmouth.
(CR 109873ST)

Opposite bottom - From Hampshire across to Sussex with 'Schools' No 30901 'Winchester' emerging from the 1,318 yard Bopeep tunnel and taking the Tunbridge Wells line (the tracks to the right of the signal box are for Bexhill / Lewes). The train will shortly arrive / pass the station at West St Leonards.
(CR 312053ST)

Above - For reasons that are not reported, in the period 1952/3 'SCT' changed the film he more usually used away from Kodak. The results were not up to the standard of before, or indeed subsequently, but these three are included not least because of their interest and because they depict the 'S & D' area. In the view above No 34041 'Wilton' is coming off the Somerset & Dorset at Broadstone in July 1953 with a down local train. In the background a 'Q' class having arrived from Ringwood / Wimborne blows off steam whilst waiting for the line to clear.
(SD287)

Opposite top - The approach to Midford. The pairing of a '2P' and 'Black 5' again on a northbound passenger train in July 1952.
(CR 312049ST)

Opposite bottom - This time the combination is of a '2P' piloting a 'West Country', No 34041 'Wilton'. The pairing seen leaving Windsor Hill tunnel northbound in July1953. The signal box seen was the only one of the S &D route to be constructed entirely of stone and dated from 1892 when this section was doubled. It formerly controlled access to Hamwood Quarry and the Mendip Granite & Asphalt Company, the buildings for the former being seen on the left. The associated sidings were out of use from 1948 but not removed until 1957.
(CR 312050ST)

Opposite page - Ancient and modern at Eastleigh in August 1954. Seen are Brighton 'Terrier' 'Boxhill', and former Southampton Docks (ex Hawthorn Leslie) 0-4-0T No 30458 'Ironside'. The latter engine was then 64 years old and had arrived at Eastleigh for scrap having been finally employed as shed pilot at Guildford. Diesel shunter No 13010 had been built at Derby in December 1952 and was renumbered D3010 in June 1958. It subsequently became No 08006 when renumbered under TOPS in March 1974.
(CR 342927ST)

Above - A feast of liveries at Eastleigh in July 1948. Former LSWR 'T3' No 563 has been repainted in LSWR livery at the works ready for preservation, whilst in the background is 'T9' No 30119 (also seen earlier) and behind (according to SCT) an unidentified 'Battle of Britain', the latter in experimental light green livery without yellow lines.
(CR 312065ST)

Opposite top - 'P' class No 31556 shunting coal on Kingston Wharf, Shoreham in July 1957.
(BRS 763)

Opposite bottom - Reconstruction of the viaduct at Redbridge (west of Southampton) in 1966. No 35019 'French line CGT' is heading an up passenger service and is cautiously threading its way through what is actually the yard associated with Redbridge Sleeper Works, the main running lines being alongside with the route to Romsey diverging to the right. The more usual, for the time, steam occupant at Redbridge, a USA tank, reposes in the shed.
(CR 109876ST)

Above - Still at Redbridge but a few years earlier (and before the tenure of the 'USA' class), 'C14' 0-4-0T No 30589 is engaged in shunting in September 1953. An example of the sharp curves necessitating short wheelbase tank engines can be seen,
(CR 308799ST)

Page 110, top - The end for a 'Schools' at the back of Eastleigh in 1963. This was possibly No 30908 'Westminster'.
(CR 312051ST)

Page 110, bottom - Former LBSCR 'A1' class 0-6-0T No 83 'Earlswood' at the back of Eastleigh in 1949 awaiting scrap. The engine has been withdrawn in 1939 and after a decade of donating spare parts was finally scrapped in 1949. The subsequent corrosion has allowed a wonderful glimpse of former LBSCR livery.
(CR 312064ST)

Page 111, top - Former 'E1R' 0-6-2T No 32094 being stripped of anything useful prior to final cutting. Eastleigh works, 1955.
(CR 312061ST)

Page 111, bottom - Another casualty an 'N15X', once No 32328 and named 'Hackworth' being dismantled outside the back of Eastleigh works. Eastleigh South signal box on the line to Fareham and Gosport is in the background.
(CR 312060ST)

Spray painting of a 4COR unit in corporate blue within the carriage works at Eastleigh in July 1966. The wheel had come full circle for SCT, he had first been employed as a Progress Chaser at the carriage works between 1934 and 1936, a time when the 4COR units were being built. Now after 30 years of steam he was back, this time chasing a new generation of electric units. (CR 23237ST)

A relic from the past, recorded at Eastleigh in July 1966. The body is from an ex LCDR passenger brake van, 27 feet long to SR diagram No 878. The last of the type were withdrawn from general service in 1935 and whilst the specific identity of this particular vehicle is not known the original SR van numbers were from 390 to 417. The vehicles were built from 1878 to 1886. This particular example had been grounded by at least 1948. (CR 109887ST)

(Notes by Mike King.)